White Lies

Crystal Stone

Fernwood
PRESS

White Lies

©2025 by Crystal Stone

Fernwood Press
Newberg, Oregon
www.fernwoodpress.com

All rights reserved. No part may be reproduced
for any commercial purpose by any method without
permission in writing from the copyright holder.

Printed in the United States of America

Cover and page design: Mareesa Fawver Moss
Cover art: Claire T. via Unsplash

ISBN 978-1-59498-162-3

This poetry book contains themes and depictions of sensitive topics, including but not limited to:

- Suicide
- Mental health struggles
- Sexual assault
- Domestic violence

Readers who may find these subjects distressing are advised to proceed with caution. Your well-being is important. If you need support, consider reaching out to a trusted friend, family member, or mental health professional.

Contents

Acknowledgments 9
Introduction with ~~Unreliable~~ Maternal Narration 11

I. 13
   By a Creek in Boyertown, PA 14
   Cento Raising Herself 15
   Endangered 16
   After Heartbreak 17
   Elegy with a Stubborn Past 18
   Preparing for Court: A Floor Plan, 924 Burke Street 19
   In the Spiritual Residue of the House 20
   Wall Art, Reframed 21
   After Mom's Death 22
   Stepdad Cento with Two Dead Wives 23
   Dad Cento 24
   Does the Environment Tell Stories, or Do We? 25
   My Friend Tells Me Talking to Me Is Like Living 26
   Fourth Grade, at the Cafeteria,
      Planning Our Wedding 27
   Elementary Brushstrokes 28
   Star Struck 29

No More White Crayons 30
Fortune Teller 31
Watching a Man Examine the Prehistoric Human
    Skeleton in the Window of the
    Conference Room I'm In 32
Brother Cento 33
TABLE 1 34
Diagnosis: Geode 36
Thinking I Can Drive after Clearing
    the Snow off Only My Windshield 37
At the Concert, My Glass Sweats On 38
When I First Meet My Paternal Grandaunt as an Adult,
    She Tells Me My Favorite Family Recipe Came
    from Their Childhood Maid, ... 39
Pennsylvania Prolonged 41
Step-mom Cento-Sonnet 42
Nutrition Facts 43
Gaslit or Coal? 44
Fraternal Twin Centos 45
Thanksgiving Break 46
Sunrise Pantoum with a Shrinking Sister 48

II. 49
    Exploring Karma Haibun 50
    If I Die Alone, I Will Die Happy 51
    Farmers Market 52
    Attractions—Exit 27 53
    Middle School 54
    Poem for February 55
    Moving On Haibun 57
    Self-Portrait as Prairie Restoration 58
    Single Woman Floor Plan,
        No Pets—740 Sweinhart Road 59
    Foraging as an Adult in my Hometown 60
    Inheritance 61
    Teaching Years 62
    Favorite Ex-Boyfriend Cento 63

Self Portrait as Snapple Facts...................................64
First Date..65
After Saturn's Return..66
Comfort Zone..67
Pulling Feathers...68
Perseids...69
Dating Toxic Masculinity 70
Conspiracy Theory...72

Notes 73
Title Index..75
First Line Index 79

Acknowledgments

Thanks to the editors of the following journals in which these poems originally appeared, often in earlier forms:
"Pennsylvania Prolonged," *Serotonin Magazine*
"Perseids," *Ruminate Magazine*
"When I First Meet My Grandaunt," *Barren Magazine*
"First Date." *Bending Genres*
"Nutrition Facts" and "Fortune Teller," *Black Telephone Magazine*
"At a Creek in Boyertown, PA," *Telepoem Booth Project*
"Sunrise Pantoum with a Shrinking Sister," *Lyrical Iowa*

Introduction with ~~Unreliable~~ Maternal Narration

Mom told us the story of the family that raised her mother. The Cody family, descendants of Buffalo Bill. *We're related*, she told us. *And Buffalo Bill married an Indian, so we're Indian, too.* She enrolled us in "Indian Guides" at the local YMCA. We made our own "coup sticks" to measure our growth. My brother's was shaped like a lightning bolt, painted yellow. Mine was blue or pink, with feathers or glitter, maybe both. I don't remember what mine looked like. I don't remember myself.

We bought dreamcatchers from Six Flags every year. I hang the only one I have left on the jewelry box on my dresser now that my mom is dead. Maybe the webs remember.

Her father, my Poppy, fought in WWII for the Americans. *Do you speak German?* they asked. *Nein*, he replied on his way to the Pacific Theater. He was a cook. He loved the war. He always thought the U.S. did such a good job. His wife, Carol, told everyone to avoid bringing up the war. We all did, except him.

My mom told me she grew up on a boat. Her siblings, too—two sisters and a brother. I never asked what really happened. My family might be reading. I can't say.

My cousin says Mom became an alcoholic after she was mugged. Her sister didn't find out until we missed checkout at the hotel. The housekeeper unlocked the door. My mom was unconscious. My brother and I were occupying ourselves.

We moved in with my aunt until I told them my cousin's brother asked me to touch his peepee. They said he doesn't use that language; stop lying. They didn't allow us to stay there.

We moved in with Poppy and Grandmom. I called my cousin often. *I'm lonely. I miss you*, I'd tell them. They thought I was fine. *You didn't know the difference between whether your grandparents had left the room or the house.*

The last time my mom was happy was in Tahiti before she met my father. Even there, she wore white, hands clasped on a crab. I can't be sure. She laughed at the cooking shows, too, but it wasn't joy.

Poppy loved his wife. For every landscape she painted, he built a frame. Every season, they changed the paintings to match the time.

The neighborhood was populated with the Germans released from the Florida internment camps. *You could order anything in German or English after the war*, my Poppy said. *But now, things have changed.*

One of my mother's sisters said Poppy was never fluent in German—he just knew a few choice words. That's not what he told me. It never is.

I.

By a Creek in Boyertown, PA

He sees two geese still on the pond
for too long: decoys. He gives
up on stillness. He tries to find another
park, but people are everywhere.
He practices instead. Dad pulls
the wooden call from his pocket, holds
the air in his hands. His hands move
in different rhythms like he knows
the alphabet of welcome. Each shape
of his fingers, their placement, changes
the length of the cluck, honk, hoot—
determines whether a murmur or a moan
is drawn out. *Who-it? Who-it? Who-it?*

The geese come in a V above our heads.
"It's so cool they came," he tells me
as we follow the dog into the woods.
Her tongue grows longer the more she jumps,
hanging from her teeth like a limp bird.
He tells me to watch for people
in orange, so we don't interrupt
their hunt. "How do you know,"
I ask, "which call makes them come closer
and which warns them of danger?"
He's still watching the dog jump,
dreaming. "I don't," he says slow,
his hands resting in his pockets.

Cento Raising Herself

When I am close enough, I am reminded
only the dead can be
still. I call back:
All the stars are cowards.
The rain has more than one face.
The spirits are not fooled.
I am my mother's bewildered shadow
waking from the house of my earliest dreams.
Sometimes she loved us. Sometimes herself
which taught us language. Things of day and of night.
And love, even when it's guttural,
will make you ugly. I answer:
The room is red, like ourselves
willing to bum in the apartment
and there's no proof I had ever lived there.
Besides, I am too beautiful.
At the time, I believed that love meant
your questions persist, like the scent
around the streetlights in Paris.
I am here, and there is no mother, no smiling sun.
When I try, I see the white cloud of her hair
through the veil of night.
No one's body could be that light.
Even if I'd been there, even if I'd touched her face,
and I stood there every day of the year,
my mother was absent. They do that, the dying.
I am sure of little, but death is like an ill-fitted suit,
a smattering of stars you fix.

Endangered

Every year, in winter, I hear the same sounds
and remember them differently. I wasn't always
comfortable staying at home, listening.
Tires spinning on icy snow, a gritty *whoosh*
that sounds more like *where* in the throat
of a grieving mouth. Tires so fast
they could be giving off heat or years.

I think less about killing myself now, more
about staying alive longer—more vegetables,
fewer shots, more steps. At the hospital, my sister
learns new ways to die. She watches the nurses save
a girl whose face bulged blue veins as the bedsheets
choked her neck. Then, that same girl ripped
an ice pack open with her teeth and drank the blue

her face once was. Always saved but never cured.
"I wonder how that girl is doing," my sister says
as she grabs another seltzer. Each day she finds
new ways to empty. We lock up more and more
of the house: razors, aspirin, bobby pins. The lock box
collects, grows. She shrinks, talks about the others
she met in her accumulating stays. Once, she laughs,

she met a cannibal. Now, time is a cannibal; it eats
itself slowly. Like her these days in the residual
nightmare of an electrocuted body, lithium,
starvation. Time doesn't care what is displaced,
who sleeps without a bed, what's ultimately lost.
Every year, I acquire more than what fits
in my suitcase, and the seltzer fizzles louder
than the birds who fly off, sounding
a call like a wet kiss, a squeaking wheel.

After Heartbreak

We make do
with what we can find.
We corkscrew the center,
smoke from an apple
with a plastic straw.

At the bar later,
I brag about everything
I could handle, show
strangers the videos
we made when we still felt

whole. I'll watch
the snow melt
from a drafty window
of a restless highway.
I won't miss him but the ritual

of it. The long walk we took
where he admitted he went
farther than he would've
alone. Someone new
will tell me he wants

to take his time,
and I'll still rush him along.
In the light of the stage,
I'll see through
his hair to the baldness

beneath. His shirt will
wrinkle like skin, hide
the muscles I'd find
he had below the translucent
heart of a knit v-neck.

Elegy with a Stubborn Past

as we wheeled Mommom
from chemo
she looked me dead
in the eye, a burning
cigarette between her lips.
How is the house? she asked,
red lipstick on the white,
as if her lungs could be
swept, the tumor
                          vacuumed

before dinner made ready.
I never met her mother,
but she died young—
an oral cancer, too. Her hair
a smokestack of curls.
She never met her mother either
because she was adopted.
Hold onto your mother.
Reach for the smoke.
                        Blow your own

rings instead. My heritage is
a hospital with fire in its lips
by the door. We don't know
how the tobacco fields grew. *Pumpkin,*
she told me, *I'll get my own water.*
My grandmother is a half-full glass
of wine. Her mother a whiskey.
My own a dresser of empty bottles,
a bed with unkempt hair,
                        piss, and shit.

Preparing for Court: A Floor Plan, 924 Burke Street

after Fatimah Asghar

Patio: Every day I watch my Poppy's beer can planes. What if mom's bottles would fly away, too?		**TV Room**: There's a map with all the places my grandparents have gone together pinned and a shelf full of succulents.
Kitchen: I'm hungry, but no one believes me. Mom said she fed us.	**Bathroom**: I drop my new ring in the toilet.	Grandmom is watching ice skating. Poppy is in the shop.
The corded phone sits by the clock on the wall.	**Hallway**: Mom scolds me. I should know better.	**Bedroom 1**: The walls are pink and there's an air conditioner, but only the grandparents are allowed in.
Living Room: Mom isn't conscious. *C'mon, we have to find it. Distract her. I'll make you dinner.* I'm not sure what will happen if she knows we found her bottles again.	**Stairwell**	**Bedroom 2**: We sit on the floor by red prayer candles. Cross legged, hands folded. My mom's face is soft in the light.
Garden: Are the sunflowers a good place to hide? I miss my dad.		

In the Spiritual Residue of the House

my stepmom sees all three of her sleeping children
writhe in positions of bondage as she prays over them

alone. In every house we've ever lived, there has been
spiritual residue holding them and a cleansing. *No ransom,*

my dad says when my sister refuses to eat. *The last girl
who lived here drank bleach, hoping to die. Now my baby keeps*

trying to kill herself, too, she says, calls the pastor. She still imagines
she could grow old here, in this Cold-War-era home, with the flag

pole in the front, a dying daughter in the bedroom. Tolstoy says,
happy families are all alike; every unhappy family is unhappy

in its own way. In a version of this poem, someone in the family
is Anna Karenina. *All endings are unhappy in their own way,*

another says. In every version, something is risked,
someone is lost. My father tries but accepts what comes:

if this is what she wants, she'll eventually succeed. There's nothing
romantic about love—any kind. This is the product. I come home

to a man who shakes in bed every time he dreams. There,
he becomes insane. Is the spiritual residue in me, my bedsheets,

my white walls? Loneliness takes more energy
than love. In one version of the poem, I believe this.

Wall Art, Reframed

Poppy died last year, so now I re-frame the landscapes, the stories.
I've never seen this place except for in the painting my
   grandmother made.
I make new memories. There, I draw a tent,
two lovers. The breeze is not a kiss but a gentle breath.

After Mom's Death

after Elizabeth Acevedo

When the phone rang,
does the cactus feel parched without sun,

she never asked even though she knew
how forgetful I've always been

with the things I love. The last time
I saw my mom, the cooking show

flamed. It wasn't a body.
By the time we found her,

her vomit no longer star-dusted
the bed. Her husband assured us,

I am escaping. The police let him
go. He cleaned up the alcohol bottles,

washed her urine from the bedsheets.
Later, he sent a letter. My brother balled

a fist. I opened my fingers
wearing her wedding rings. I will

never forget my stepdad's toothless smile,
Mom's stuffed mushrooms

mashed between his gums.

Stepdad Cento with Two Dead Wives

Some are willing to trust any anchor—
their paternal regard. My stepdad
was hunched vintage, a nighttime,
a trembling brittleness,
a noose dangling from a tree limb,
making shadows—
things that are worse than death.
He was already old when our mom took him in
the sewage of his body.
Blessed are those who can distract themselves.
If one could have seen it from above,
peeked out over the ragged lip
of the cutlery. How would he handle it?
Dearest Father, what becomes of the woman?
I've been steaming away, thin.
Isn't this the history you want?
Say it: the tree is sick. Love is far.
He sees himself in pastels, neatly groomed,
the toothless wonder,
laughing into the teeth of death.
Yes, he says. *It's a good day to be above ground!*
When I return to that house, I eat the food. The days
have been growing raw. There is fire left.
I would do a lot of things—
if only a bewildered kid—
so I alone could see the beast push.
Not the bitterness, not the lifting,
but the weight.
His hands shake. His drugged face blurs—
drenched, adrift and unhappy in the vast ocean—
the break between this bitter world:
an open space
where nothing is enough.

Dad Cento

You were the window.
In the legend you were delivered,
as if it were some noble thing—
the mustached man laying dollars down,
with fishgut and Marlboro's, everyone cheering.
Summer seemed to bloom against the will
of ancient trenches, highways,
the faint, almost fantastic
hoof-prints through the long grass.
You could be anyone's father, found,
body trapped in this backcountry that bleeds.
A drizzled white floods everywhere we think we know
about, the world unzipping
that color. To you, what was solid was miraculous.
Our time is brief. Summer is over.
How to make it bigger, I say, remembering,
sleeves rolled and hand shading your face—looking.
You swore to be protector. After a swollen breeze,
we played dolls in that house where you staggered
with conversation, raised just enough
to calm an angry ocean
in my heart like a starving deserter.
Here is the comfort of familiar shadows:
in your silhouette, I can see myself.
Like puffs of smoke, like a bright moon.
A poet burning his life's work,
and you, at the center, finding something real.
The poem for the world includes all the letters of your name

Does the Environment Tell Stories, or Do We?[1]

At the party, I'm a jukebox. One shot of tequila, another story. A White Claw, a botched sex narrative. A cup of wine, here is the sadness.

Poppy's always laughing, even when he tells stories that aren't funny. Every time I see him, he tells me he's another year older whether or not a year has passed. He's getting old, so is his memory.

The family tells me he remembers things wrong. I wonder if he just started talking about the truths. Grandmom told me she didn't know he could cook for years into their marriage. But that's what he did in the war. What else was he hiding? How much more didn't we know?

At my dad's family parties, I'm a drag. I talk too much about myself. The Phillies are on. The Eagles are on. I'd rather watch an eagle nesting in a tree. I do nothing, but I think too much.

I'm reading about the German-American camps that I thought were another one of my mom's family myths. Krammer says, "...the first casualty of war is Truth... " I keep re-writing that.

The first casualty ~~of war~~ of birth is Truth
The first ~~casualty~~ mutation ~~of war~~ of inheritance is Truth
~~The~~ Our first casualty ~~of war~~ is Truth
The first ~~casualty of war is~~ Truth
~~The~~ Our first ~~casualty of war is~~ Truth

---

[1] In *America's Invisible Gulag,* Fox cites Peter and Leni Gillman saying, "Bluntly stated, the United States asked Britain how to do it." American politicians had no precedent for interning during WWI and WWII so they asked their parents in the British parliament for help. Do we ever stop looking to our parents as role models, even when they're doing something wrong?

My Friend Tells Me Talking to Me Is Like Living

a Gertrude Stein poem, which is to say
she doesn't understand me, the way she doesn't

understand walking birds. She chases them
until they fly. *You have wings, use them! Get out*

of here. I pick violets for the lemonade I'll stir
after our walk. We've had nothing before,

so we use everything—the sprouting garlic,
the drying onion, weeds on the side of the road

growing among cigarettes and discarded Red Bulls.
If I had wings, I would never walk,

which is to say we think we could do better
with what the cardinal has if we had more. I think

about how I've smelled skunks my whole life
but never seen them. How we're all hiding

behind some odorous fear. Maybe it's not just walking
that slows us down but this: the gap between

what we have and what we choose, what we know
and what we do, the placement

of hope on an open country road where
the toads are asking for sex, and the birds are grounded

picking discards they find instead of enjoying
the view they could have from the trees.

Fourth Grade, at the Cafeteria, Planning Our Wedding

We were all planetary, too—
like our favorite manga, chasing
a legendary diamond, a man
who'd be our moons, orbiting us
like rings. We made plans:
an invite list without space
for his friends. A bridal party
split along best friend lines:
Tori would be my maid of honor,
Oksana could have Monique
or Bhuvana. We would all be
brides' maids. My dress
strapless, Tori's with lace. We
even drew the rings—they
looked like frosted eyes that
never learned to blink.

Elementary Brushstrokes

Sun steeped in a cup of sky:
we, too, had the option to
blend in. Everyone around me knew
where they were from:
HaYoung sent me lollipops
from Korea when she went
back home. Juliet went
to Ukraine school in the evenings.
Bhuvana ate Indian food
that we teased her for. I ate butter
and cheese sandwiches
with a Capri-Sun. I was this deer
in the evening, looking at all the trees
that know their roots.

Star Struck

I look most like Sailor Jupiter, but I only have brown eyes. I wish my eyes were green like hers, my dad's, and my brother's. I just had to look like my mom. I even got her nose.

Sailor Pluto is the most mysterious character. She rarely shows up. I only remember her in one episode: her nearly black skirt. Her long green hair. I am green, too, and young. I lack her confidence, but I'm not quite as clumsy as Sailor Moon. I never wanted to be her—I just wanted her powers.

The boy next door has Stone Cold Steve Austin figurines. He brings them over, and we play in the sandbox. I have Sailor Moon's staff, but it's pink, so I leave it inside.

We always hang out but only outside. I wasn't allowed to have friends inside. We didn't know how my mom would be.

Poppy might watch from the patio, between the planes he made out of old beer cans, my Grandmom's wall decorations made out of the funnies from the Sunday paper, and the glass container with the shells she collected from every one of their travels. Tidy and labeled. An eccentric porch with concrete floors.

Many times they would be busy. Grandmom by the TV, painting or out bowling. Poppy in his wood shop, making bird feeders.

I watch Sailor Moon while my mom is unconscious on the couch. I never tell anyone, but I have a crush on Sailor Venus until I meet Sailor Neptune. I would kiss her, too.

No More White Crayons

White crayons, he says as we wake. *White
men*, I say, throwing him off. Valerie Solanas

would've finished the line, *are a bore. Aren't functional*,
he continued. I explain, *but they work on black paper.*

He says, *every other color works, too.*
This is how it starts: how we begin to decide

what deserves a place in our pictures,
how we begin to re-negotiate ourselves.

He thinks our late-night philosophies
will lead to sex. Tonight, they don't.

But I like his red highlights, waxy ringlet
curls. The way they stay in place when he lies

in bed, calls his mother in the morning after
he orgasms. Her breakfast is Mountain Dew

and a cigarette, a lit white crayon that shrinks.
On rainy days, the sky is a white crayon

on gray paper clouds, melting into raindrops.
On every white page scribbled in white

crayon there is a rutted message: like *I wish
I was able to love you the same way*, or

I wish the earth didn't have any moons.

Fortune Teller

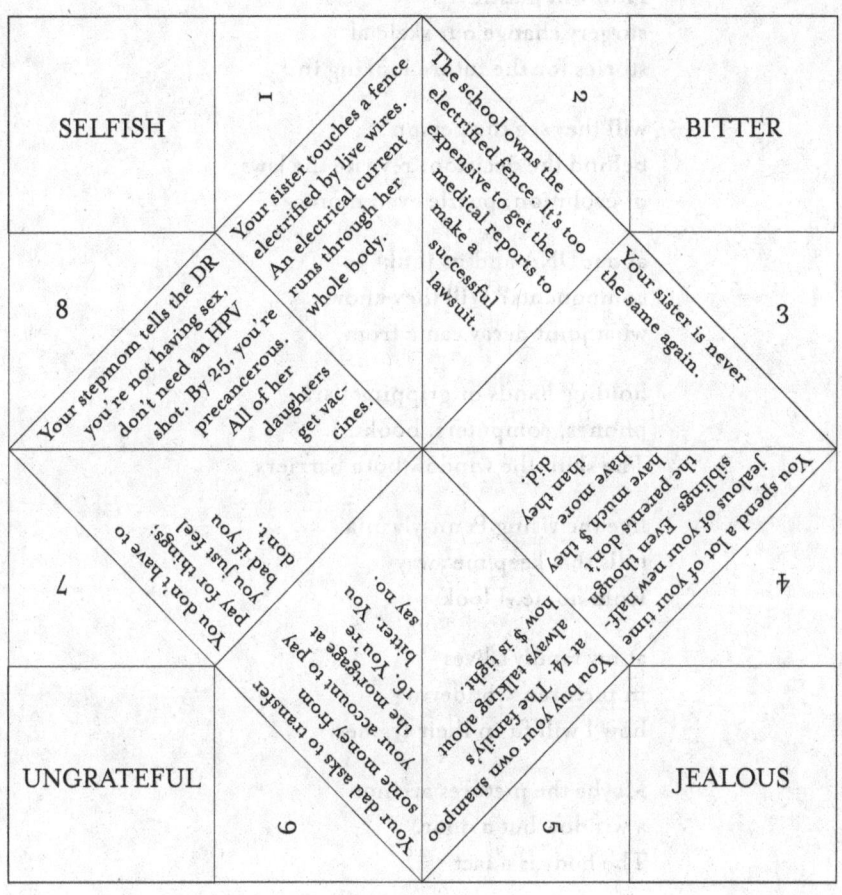

SELFISH			BITTER
	1	2	
8			3
7			4
	6	5	
UNGRATEFUL			JEALOUS

1. Your sister touches a fence electrified by live wires. An electrical current runs through her whole body.

2. The school owns the electrified fence. It's too expensive to get the medical reports to make a successful lawsuit.

3. Your sister is never the same again.

4. You spend a lot of your time jealous of your new half-siblings. Even though the parents don't have much $ they have more than they did.

5. You buy your own shampoo at 14. The family's always talking about how $ is tight. You're bitter. You say no.

6. Your dad asks to transfer some money from your account to pay the mortgage at 15.

7. You don't have to pay for things; you just feel bad if you don't.

8. Your stepmom tells the DR you're not having sex, don't need an HPV shot. By 25, you're precancerous. All of her daughters get vaccines.

31

Watching a Man Examine the Prehistoric Human Skeleton in the Window of the Conference Room I'm In

How will plastic
surgery change our skeletal
stories for the future looking in:

will they see the person
behind the decision, rewrite the laws
of evolution, puzzle even more

about DNA and its junk
components? Will they know
what joint decay came from

holding hands or gripping bars,
phones, computers, books.
The skin, the window both barriers

like the rising Pennsylvania
tolls that keep me away
from home. I look

at my family's lives
in pictures, wondering
how I will fit in their frames.

Maybe the pictures are not
a window but a door.
The body is a fact

or a story. Maybe he was just
looking at his own reflection, the shape
of the skeleton in his eyes.

Brother Cento

Whole and indivisible. A stone pillar
chipped and blistered with stars.
He was too young to be alone in the yard.
Men like this are molded. From need. From
want. Sacred, there's always a woman
trying to balance on slick rocks.
There's a point where it all gets still.
The sea current, the sound of the Sound.
Before sleep, my brother will bless himself and lie down,
willing not only to receive but to bestow a kindness.

TABLE 1

Analysis of Levels of Parentification[1]

Individual Development *Ontogeny*	Proximal Settings *Microsystem*	Distal Settings *Exosystem*

Parental Attachment:
  Disordered (M)
  Secure (D)
 	
Privation
  Inconsistent
 	
Child:
  Avoidant
  Anxious
  Attachment
 	
Angry, Fits
Outbursts
Inconsolable
 	
Self-Schemas
Self-Differentiation
Capacity to Care
	Family Stressors
	  Alcohol
	  Money
	  Time
	  Boundaries
	
	Peers
	  Disabled BFF
	  Other Languages
	  Other Customs
	  Other Religions
	  Married Parents
	
	Teachers
	  "wow, your life seems so hard!"
	
	Role Induction:
	  what is a sister?
	  daughter?
		Neighborhood:
		  Hollywood, PA
		  Lansdale, PA
		  King of Prussia, PA
		  Myrtle Beach, SC
		  Detroit, MI
		
		Paternal Employment:
		  Bookkeeper
		  Hospitality
		  Management

1 Chart remade and personalized from Gregor Jurkovic's *Lost Childhoods: The Plight of the Parentified Child*.

Interrelation of Settings *Mesosystem*	Cultural Consistencies *Macrosystem*	Ethical Context *Co-Being*
Home—School Parent—Peer Parent—Parent Maternal Side—Paternal Side Teacher—Student	Parental Education Societal Attitudes Gender Roles Social Legitimacy	Entitlement

*Note: The various settings are viewed from the perspective of the child.

Diagnosis: Geode

Was I born the mineral
or stone? Hoarse
voice or eyes?

I'm trying to fit
inside the jaded edges
of an open story

we're all still weathered
weathering and not
entirely transparent.

Thinking I Can Drive after Clearing the Snow off Only My Windshield

As soon as I stop, everything I hadn't
cleared fell from the rooftop and blocked

my view. My therapist asks, *when
will you forgive yourself?* I consider

telling her how my friend's snake
squeezed a fart from the mouse it devoured,

how there is something funny in every tragedy.
Avoidant, she'd write in the session notes

or say aloud as I left for another walk in the snow.
At the military academy, my dad got beat

with socks full of soap for mouthing off
because everyone had to do more

push-ups than they could handle. In place of a lock,
he disassembled a hair dryer—to protect himself,

made the doorknob electric to touch. He's always
remembered better than he remembers.

We share a hit as we walk, and I know
I am my father's daughter. The last time

I left home, a toddler in the airport said hi
relentlessly. If I didn't listen closely enough,

it was hard to tell if she said *hi* or *bye*. The only
difference between the words is the way the mouth opens.

At the Concert, My Glass Sweats On

my poems. The flies are more interested
in water than whiskey. It doesn't matter
how many; I've forgotten
how to pray. I see summer
as the final note, leaves a coffin.
The sun has not yet dressed
for the wake. I always wear black
when the clothes I like are
in the wash. I let the bug die
on its back when it falls on me.
My yard hasn't had grass since
the landlord ripped up the sidewalks.
I haven't driven on a sidewalk
since I delivered pizzas in a town
the same name as my brother.
How many siblings do you have
left? Do they lie, too,
like a carpet patterned with tears?

When I First Meet My Paternal Grandaunt as an Adult, She Tells Me My Favorite Family Recipe Came from Their Childhood Maid,

shows me the picture,
excitedly. *Here we are,*

the four of us. Growing
up, Dad told us

each peach carries
a flavor and texture

unclear from the skin's color
alone. To know the truth

about the sweetness or sour,
we ate a slice of each open-faced

peach cake made in celebration
of his birthday. We called

the recipe Mommom's.
We were wrong

about what to name
what we ate. I have since

betrayed expectation, too.
The last time

I kissed a man, I thought
about a woman whose breasts

were so close to my own
in bed, who I wanted to hold

but didn't, my body pressed
against the wall instead

of her back. To be always
facing a wall. To be

always out of touch,
velvet wetting silent

tongues. I know now
everything is

an accumulation: kisses,
kids, cakes, pounds,

lies. Like them, I've been
dishonest about who I am.

Pennsylvania Prolonged

The sun has a tantrum, throws
shade and the clouds are just dirty

laundry in the room of the sky.
Lock eyes with the lingering

blue. Watch how the unforgiving
trees never face the sun.

God is only a wind-thrown
punch, downed red pills

in the sunset's open mouth.
If it could speak, the sun would

stay silent, fade—make
way for the rising moon.

Step-mom Cento-Sonnet

My mom puts on make up, and she is not my mom.
Every Sunday morning, something's wrong—
at her heart is a stopped clock.
If, from a centuried window, she looks out,
she clings to me.
Never give a woman more sadness than she needs.
Rain. A steady drizzle.
Outside the dream, songbirds fall from the trees.
While wet nose deep in the lilies, she'd miss
the trees shoot up straight,
the cicadas grind their teeth.
That little beauty existed in our yard,
and sometimes, there would be story
to become me.

Nutrition Facts
7 servings per household

1 body

Amount per day
Trauma   00

% Daily Value*

Total Fat 60kg   Strong, Loud
   Saturated Fat 5kg   Bitter
   Trans Fat 2kg   Self Lies
Cholesterol 3kg   Poems
Sodium 200g   Whole Body
Total Carbohydrates 60kg   Family Lies
Sugars >1g   No sweetness added
Proteins 20kg   Silence

*The % daily value tells you how much a nutrient contributes to a daily body. An average American body consumes an unknown amount of tra disappear, weekly.

INGREDIENTS: depression, self-harm, binge, stop, punish, exercise, more, lift heavier, hide, disappear disappear, disappear

Gaslit or Coal?

My dad loves giving gifts, making the people he loves happy. He spent months tracking down Sailor Moon toys I'd love. They were hard to find, overseas or expensive. He got them anyway, but they were ones Mom already found.

Mom gets coal from a gift shop in a small town we visited when she was drunk. She put it in our stockings at Christmas. She laughed when we opened it and then gave us other things we really wanted.

The judge doesn't believe us, no matter what we show her. *How do you know to call the cops? Who's telling you what those bottles are?*

Over time, I choose to undermine myself over and over again when I give my opinions. I ask for advice when I don't need it. People learn not to trust me. I don't even trust myself.

Fraternal Twin Centos

I.

My mother's grief
was true. A thousand degrees, not just boiled—
I picture a heart lying down on the floor
in a pile near the shed where mourning
can't decide what's fake and what's fact.
How surreal it is to
be lost in what we must call a pastiche.
How to start clean. This love even sits up.

II.

With some glee or abandon, the clatter
slung like new moons. Her perfect bean toes
group themselves as if in a painting.
I want the colors—unstuck, unblurred,
the fields have eroded and the sky
face flashing free. Child-arms
such a soft, feathery thing could make the morning bleed.

Thanksgiving Break

The kids eat boredom like snacks.

I tell the gold digger who married my poppop too much
about my life. She pretends she's interested.
In my stories, not him.

I pray to a picture of my late mom
mom. "If you're listening and see this,
haunt that bitch."

My parents say I can't bench press
my youngest sister. They donated
the old machines. I want nice shoulders.

I mistake the dogs barking next door
for my stomach growling. The sound is faint. I'm not
in touch with my body. I eat

leftover pizza every day
in the breezeway. The oldest of my sisters
won't touch it. She doesn't like the way food feels

in her stomach. We drink well
water. More likely to be contaminated,
my stepmom says it tastes better.

I feel like a false prophet when I teach my grandfather
about the Trail of Tears and my sisters about immigrant children.
Fox News tells it different.

The girls are growing up. They stopped flushing
tampons. They even made
a sign. "Toeilets" is spelled wrong.

My dad is so mad he raised
feminists. Autocorrect changes "sonnet"
to "dinner." Even my phone is

tired of hearing about work. I go outside.
Smoke from the California fires
reaches the Pennsylvania sky.

Sunrise Pantoum with a Shrinking Sister

Everything looks bigger in the winter:
the bus fuller with the inflated body
of coats, hats that grow heads taller than hair.
Beautiful stacks of snow pushed aside liberate

the bus fuller with the inflated body
I still carry. Even the smoke looks
beautiful. Like stacks of snow pushed aside. Liberate
the memory of hills she and I sledded together

that I still carry. Even the smoke looks
ordinary in the camera's lens. I try to capture
the memory of hills we sledded together,
even the pink streaking strands of clouds

ordinary in the camera's lens. I try to capture,
but everything is yellowed here—
even the pink streaking strands of clouds.
Sometimes people tell me I look lighter now,

but everything is yellowed here—
on coats, hats that grow heads taller than hair.
Sometimes people tell me I look lighter now,
but everything looks bigger in the winter.

II.

Exploring Karma Haibun

I think about the way Jess found Greg's body dead in front of my building. We were all looking, always too late. *Nam-myoho-renge-kyo.* My own Poppy laughed before the first time he turned his gun inward. The family took a cruise to avoid the truth. *Nam-myoho renge-kyo.* We don't even know the cues. *Nam-myoho-renge-kyo.* Over lunch after my first car accident, my godmother told me, your mother loved you so much. I waited until she left to cry. *Nam-myoho-renge-kyo.* No one loves me, Auntie A, I thought. Not even me. I left my keys at the gay club and woke up on the concrete after throwing up blue curacao in the bushes next to my door. *Nam-myoho-renge-kyo.* She still sends me the same frying pan every year on my birthday. Personality is a karma, too, I'm told. That's why I have more spatulas than spoons, why I try to deadlift more than my weight even though I feel my fingers threatening to snap. *Nam-myoho-renge-kyo.* I won't give up, even if it kills me. *Nam-myoho-renge-kyo.* It might kill me. *Nam-myoho-renge-kyo.* All of us trying to hate ourselves independent of our regard for each other. *Nam-myoho-renge-kyo.* I met Anna in a leopard-print bra at 6 am, emerging from the curtains in the hallway bathroom. We've been friends ever since: both early risers, taken with dandelion dew. *Nam-myoho-renge kyo.* We always blamed ourselves, even when it wasn't our fault. *Nam-myoho-renge-kyo.* I might have learned to read maps from her if I wasn't distracted with ancestral scenes. *Nam-myoho-renge-kyo.* I might have learned to say I love you and mean more than *I love the way you look at me with kindness,* or *I love the way your eyes are*

blue dandelions
with sick bees as pupils
that pollinate every bloom.

If I Die Alone, I Will Die Happy

Like the cop who gets excited
every time he finds a new bottle
of alcohol in my underaged sister's car.

The couch is a Rice Krispies Treat, takes
a bite every time we sit down.
The vape gasps and crackles like a lung.

My last date told me that he only met
his father once in middle school, beat him
with his friends, left him

bleeding in the street alone.
My sister's boyfriend makes a ring for her
from an old wrench. His love

is not symmetrical either. There's a hole
where a rock could be. It's Hidirellez,
my friend tells me. If we write our wishes

and bury them beneath a rose bush,
they'll come true. We find the pink petals
in my parents' garden a week too late,

when the holiday is over. I put the ring
on my finger when my sister isn't looking.
It fits awkwardly, like love.

Farmers Market

We fell asleep in New York, woke up
in the future. The morning cloud
cover sparkled in the reflection
of the water. By afternoon, the clouds
a gray shale, a pathway through the blue
sky. Her eyes are blue suns in the full
moon the year has been. The past low
hanging fruit, alto clef citrus, bottom shelf
vibrations. Now at the farmer's market,
even the veggies rainbow, our new world
colored in shades I've never seen
in the wild—purple, green and orange
cauliflower, pink stemmed Swiss chard,
golden beets, brown petaled sunflowers.
This isn't where we expected to find life
in Oklahoma's unpredictable hues,
but we manifested this, and the lips
of the sky will always close with a kiss.

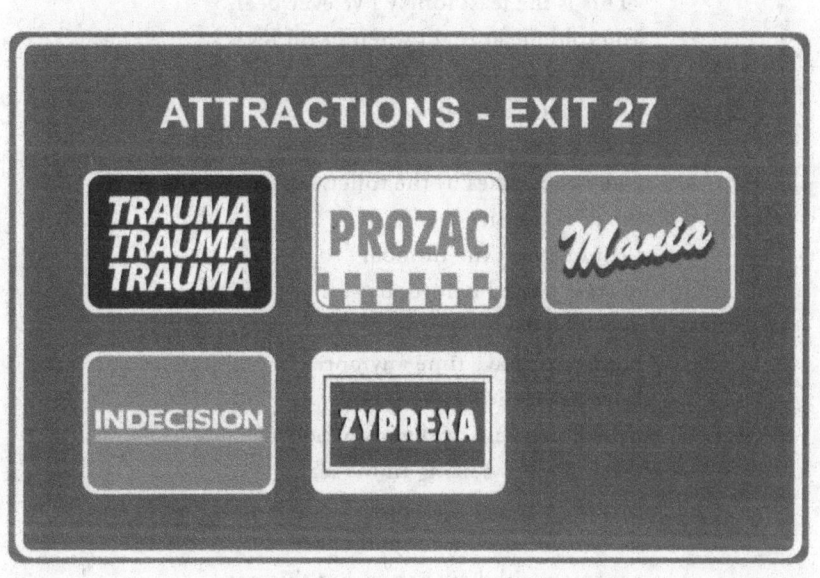

Middle School

In the back of the classroom,
the boys are throwing ladybugs
and folding paper guns.
"This is the least lonely I've ever been."
You told me at night when I said I was
empty. Now, light barely
illuminates the hallway:
slow jazz in the concert of gossip.
The sky puddles by the toilet,
the roof leaking again.
I could count the number
of stars passed before the sun
came the day I met you,
but I don't have time anymore.
Love is a braid cut
with stolen scissors by my window,
tears of a boy seizing in his seat
by the door. I don't know
how to create—I draw half a face:
a woman with hair better, but thinner,
than mine. She has no nose,
but there's nothing left to smell:
just raw sewage on the grass after rain.
Noise clouds and I drop
the picture woman on the floor,
pretend that without breath
she knows how to swim.

Poem for February

Love is a nostalgia aloof

    a roof is supposed to keep

        the rainwater out of the living

    room without effort but it's wrinkling

down get back up you told me

      it's not cool to ghost so I witch

          my hands around your waist

    in the afternoon when you let me

love your messy hair

    do the woods

        need canopy from sunlight like I do

when my mood gargoyles from affection

    to fear again when I say I miss

      you I don't mean your body but

the way your skin is smooth marble

    countertops I would make you

        pancakes if roaches weren't

hiding in the cupboards beside the spatulas

        under the plates by the glass

I broke last night because whiskey

                          makes my fingers slide down curvy

shapes in dark places I'm not

beautiful without lipstick or copper

                          eyeliner the kids think my hair

is a nappy weave   but it's real naturally

                    dark and full

        like your eyes and mine

Moving On Haibun

Bills pile like leaves. Three jobs should be enough. At the lake, the dock moves from the steps of a fisherman. She tells me she ran out of hot dogs, so she uses Slim Jims and Cheetos instead. She's nice, but I wish she never came. I'm killing bugs with my hands, watching with a beer. It's beautiful, but I know, looking around, one day I will leave this place, too. And no one will call me to see how I've been. I won't think of them either. For now, I dream of hayrides and apple orchards I won't visit until next year, hot days and bonfires in cool nights.

Mountains rising behind trees
topped with a cloudy wig
that covers their green with white.

Self-Portrait as Prairie Restoration

At first, it looks like razed trees, dying
underbrush. Goats on the hill clearing old plants.

The lake's shape isn't how you remember it.
There are new curves, edges.

Birds rest like chirping half-moons.
It's easy to ignore the mating toads.

The geese still see themselves as hissing
managers, Zamboni the waves to clear

space for their children. I will never
want that, no matter how many birdsongs.

It's louder now, even though it looks
more compact. Everything it lost came back:

grass, milkweed, and monarchs. There's no need
to climb trees. The sun is visible over the lake.

Single Woman Floor Plan, No Pets—740 Sweinhart Road

The room is a curly mind, frizzy-brain girl like me. It's got a big-nose heart, a little crooked, not most attractive. Poetry is a tourist wearing my innermost moods. It straight irons my thoughts. I pierce the skin, hang pictures like rose gold hoops from the ear of the walls.

Foraging as an Adult in my Hometown

The pupils of the purple coneflowers
are dilated. The wind blows the petals

like a wish that falls down
the grasses' dry cheeks. If truth is

beautiful, why are we always
pulling weeds whose roots last longer

than anything we plant? I eat
mulberries and wonder if the robins

have learned how to get high,
if somewhere a robin mother

is drunk on fermented berries,
listening to songs on a passing car's radio

with a dry throat, wishing it could
sing a Weezer song or just listen, for once

take a break from sending mating calls,
become radio static for an afternoon

so everyone would want to change
the channel. She could rest

without guilt, grow wild
like mushrooms without worrying

what her children and lovers
might become while she's gone,

rewriting love songs to sound
like a brass instrument

that she heard once
at a backyard barbeque, closing

her eyes, waiting on the moon.

Inheritance

At the cafe, the owner is asked
what they can do about the glare.

She suggests that they move
the table, tells them, "It's winter,

we're trying to soak up
as much of the sun as we can."

Teaching Years

In the crumbling heart
of the ceiling, there is mold

and bats. In the hallway,
a taped fountain and boil water

notice. I paint the walls blue, a bright
melancholy that soothes. I write

"Change Your Mindset" on the bulletin
board to remind the kids to keep going.

I don't believe in the sun's golden
potential or the moon's steadfast cycles.

The crumbs in my desk aren't mine.
Neither are the sticky notes, plastic

forks, paper clips, pennies and nickels,
but I use them all anyway. My lover

wants to leave because he loves
me. There is no metaphor for emptiness,

just the hollow memory
of a flooded hallway

beside my door I decorated
to read "Oh, the Places You'll Go."

Favorite Ex-Boyfriend Cento

Multidimensional, needing no introduction.
Even when it is imagined. Even when it ends.
Evicted rain—
you carry around the weight—
atlas of bone, field of muscle.
You are both earnest parent and wily child
the Lord teaches me to love without fear
in a weak moment, one of many,
from inside. Your inner map's like that—
it's a fool moon. Don't leave me alone.
All of this damage is already done.

Self Portrait as Snapple Facts

"The average dream is a nightmare"

"A full moon is always a chance for extra wishes"

"I have the introversion of an only child."

"Love mostly hurts."

First Date

He said we'd rename every dog we saw
because it's a better game than love.

I name every dog after favorite poem titles:
I call the golden, "If all of my relationships

fail, and I don't have any kids, do I even know
what love is?" He nicknames the dog

knowledge. I name the chihuahua "Fiction"
to save time. There is no nickname for fantasy.

The husky is "Things." The German
short-haired pointer is "On Being Cautioned

Against Walking on a Headland Overlooking
the Sea Because It Is Frequented by a Lunatic."

He nicknames the dog *caution*. For every word,
there is a sentence unspoken, an owner

that chooses not to revise their love daily.
Today, I rename myself "Ugly Music."

Tomorrow, I might call the dogs "You Can Take Off
Your Sweater, I've Made Today Warm."

After Saturn's Return

The trees shake loose
their pockets of change;

clouds accumulate like lint.
This is where we meet:

beside a door you built,
in a yard you don't yet own.

We cheer, share the present
like a drink. There is no music

in the house, no bark or growl
when the dog greets me

for the first time.
If we'd have looked up,

we might have seen more:
watched the copper moon

land, heads up, in the ground
of the September sky.

Comfort Zone

It seems grand—the fondue
night he planned with three courses,

the evenings in the hot tub, the trip
to Puerto Rico he promised

but never officially booked—
but they're fossils of old love lives.

Recycled intimacy. Leftover
romance. The morning dew is actually

tears precipitating in the eyes
of the daisies, and the clouds

from the power plant are hands
reaching into the lost and found bin

of the sky. Its fingers stay ringless
like the earth, sun, or moon.

Pulling Feathers

Ask the finches: what else is there
to do when you're running low?

The waning gibbous moon
empties into the nest of night,

plucking feathers from the last
full moon. I wish it were true:

that we all had feathers to spare.
The seagulls circle me like a nest

in the rhythm of oasis, champagne
supernova, like stars are grains

of sand. We fast like waves, salt
in oceans. The wind carries

finches of light, rainbows
from tears that never reach

the horizon, just settle in
unraveling threads of towel.

Perseids

The trees swab the clouds. The sky
doesn't understand the science.

Night dismisses day, returns
with spotted lanternfly wings.

What it means to be unaffected
by recent death. To have

favorable conditions to grow.
We pretend meteors are stars

that travel across the sky
instead of disappearing. We see

old light, think it's still there, trace
the past. I mistake Draco

for Orion's Belt many times,
lose track of even my own sign

on the horizon. We become
parked cars in the empty lot

like time. Each year, I age
more than I mean to, even here

in the arms of a quiet wish
beneath streaks of invasive light.

Dating Toxic Masculinity

after Morgan Parker

Toxic masculinity says that flexing
isn't superficial. Toxic masculinity says all women
play games. Toxic masculinity calls
the driver queer for driving too slow,
a cunt for cutting him off. Toxic masculinity says,
"I don't get how you call yourself queer
when I've been inside you." Toxic masculinity doesn't
eat pussy. He "got over it" when he was younger.
Toxic masculinity says, "Poets are
dicks, you're really gonna write that down?"
Toxic masculinity admires himself in bed.
He's always on top. He won't tell me I'm pretty.
He thinks I'll leave him. Toxic masculinity is
insecure but thinks he should try modeling.
He calls emotions "false" and "weakness."
He gets mean when I don't smile.
He calls me sensitive. When I make him mad,
he tells me, "Say it again, and I'll put my dick
in your butt." Toxic masculinity has tiny
nipples and hard abs. He's not comfy
to cuddle with. He smells like smoke.
He won't kiss me because I asked
him to this time. Toxic masculinity always wants
to be in control. He thinks he needs to protect
me. Toxic masculinity gets jealous of my career,
tells me he needs space, then doesn't understand
why I'm leaving. Toxic masculinity can't
make up his mind. He needs a job.
He wants to learn poetry because he hates
that I'm good at something he isn't.
Toxic masculinity is always giving me advice.
He argues with me until I say
something really mean and then says, "I got you!

That's who you *really* are." Toxic masculinity cooks
well but needs to hear it. He needs to hear
he's perfect all the time. He says he falls in love easily.
He says women always leave him. Toxic masculinity is
a self-fulfilling prophecy. I'm scared to end it
with toxic masculinity because I don't know
how he'll take it. Sometimes he's really sweet.
Sometimes he really listens. Maybe I deserve toxic
masculinity. Maybe I was hurtful, too. Toxic
masculinity takes jabs every chance he gets.
Toxic masculinity thinks it's all about him.
He wants his own poem but not *this* poem.
Toxic masculinity's friends hate me.
They think I'm arrogant. They think I'm changing
him. Toxic masculinity says "I'm sorry" but only
after he's pushed too far. I don't blame toxic
masculinity. His mom abandoned him.
He worries I'm settling with him, knows
I will leave him, too, and sometimes, toxic masculinity cries.
He tells me he wants to love me. He
says I confuse him. He confuses me, too.
Toxic masculinity isn't sleeping well without me.
He doesn't care that I am tired. He continues
telling me his problems. He wants
to be heard. He wants a hit. Toxic masculinity
was late for our first date. He brought a friend.

Conspiracy Theory

Mermaid eyes. A margarita's iridescent
scales. Love has always been
swallowed by an ocean, in a place
no one seems to locate.
Love is Malaysia Air 370, a loose
Southwest engine. I microdose
love holding my breath under water.
Reverse mermaid. The water chokes
the sun until it's just waves.
The clouds are just swelling,
bruises of the sky.

Notes

"Cento Raising Herself" sources: Diane Seuss, Terrance Hayes, Lisel Mueller, Katherine Larson, Michael Mlekoday, Tracy K. Smith, Shara McCallum, Olivia Gatwood, Donte Collins, Matty Layne Glassgow, and francine j. harris.

"Stepdad Cento with Two Dead Wives" sources: Denise Duhamel, Denise Levertov, Patricia Smith, Marcus Wicker, Shannon Bramer, Natasha Trethewey, Carl Phillips, Marvin Bell, Kaveh Akbar, Tom Andrews, Dorianne Laux, Will Schutt, Gary Dop, Reginald Dwayne Betts, Diannely Antigua, Sharon Olds, Ocean Vuong, Matthew Zapruder, Adam Zagajewski, Phil Bolsta, Joseph Fasano, Diana Khoi Nguyen and Debra Marquart

"Dad Cento" sources: Ocean Vuong, Michelle Bonczek Evory, Sharon Olds, Langston Hughes, Jacob Saenz, Marek L. Beggs, Jennifer Elise Foerster, Adam Zagajewski, Carl Dennis, Fatimah Asghar, Diana Khoi Nguyen, Diannely Antigua, Reginald Dwayne Betts, Matty Layne Glasgow, Jericho Brown, Dean Rader, Will Schutt, e.e.cummings, Patricia Smith and Tracy K. Smith

"Brother Cento" sources: Brandon Melendez, Tom Andrews, Heather Derr-Smith, Indigo Moor, Victoria Chang, Gabrielle Calvocoressi, Elise Paschen, and David Evans

"Step-mom Cento Sonnet" sources: Jose Olivarez, Lucille Clifton, Deborah Landau, Patrick Ryan Frank, A. E. Stallings, Claire Wahmanholm, Gary Soto, Rosanna Warren, James Armstrong, Sharon Olds, Shivanee Ramlochan, Jennifer L. Knox.

"Fraternal Twin Cento" sources: Erika Meitner, Halsey, Dani Tauber, Didi Jackson, Cate Marvin, Ada Limon, Keith Leonard, Kim Addonizio, Kwame Dames, Joy Katz, Lisel Mueller, Charlotte Seley, Mark Wunderlich, Adrienne Rich, Matty Layne Glasgow

"Favorite Ex-Boyfriend Cento" sources: Jessica Abughattas, Kate Baer, Pete Miller, Gina Tron, Natalie Diaz, Dylan Krieger, Kiki Petrosino, Sarah Lindsay, Catherine W. Carter, Angel Garcia, Alexandria Hall

Title Index

A
After Heartbreak 17
After Mom's Death 22
After Saturn's Return 66
At the Concert, My Glass Sweats On 38
Attractions—Exit 27 53

B
Brother Cento 33
By a Creek in Boyertown, PA 14

C
Cento Raising Herself 15
Comfort Zone 67
Conspiracy Theory 72

D
Dad Cento 24
Dating Toxic Masculinity 70
Diagnosis: Geode 36
Does the Environment Tell Stories, or Do We? 25

E
- Elegy with a Stubborn Past 18
- Elementary Brushstrokes 28
- Endangered 16
- Exploring Karma Haibun 50

F
- Farmers Market 52
- Favorite Ex-Boyfriend Cento 63
- First Date 65
- Foraging as an Adult in my Hometown 60
- Fortune Teller 31
- Fourth Grade, at the Cafeteria,
  Planning Our Wedding 27
- Fraternal Twin Centos 45

G
- Gaslit or Coal? 44

I
- If I Die Alone, I Will Die Happy 51
- Inheritance 61
- In the Spiritual Residue of the House 20
- Introduction with ~~Unreliable~~ Maternal Narration 11

M
- Middle School 54
- Moving On Haibun 57
- My Friend Tells Me Talking to Me Is Like Living 26

N
- No More White Crayons 30
- Nutrition Facts 43

P
- Pennsylvania Prolonged 41
- Perseids 69
- Poem for February 55
- Preparing for Court: A Floor Plan, 924 Burke Street 19
- Pulling Feathers 68

S

Self-Portrait as Prairie Restoration 58
Self Portrait as Snapple Facts 64
Single Woman Floor Plan, No Pets—
   740 Sweinhart Road 59
Star Struck 29
Stepdad Cento with Two Dead Wives 23
Step-mom Cento-Sonnet 42
Sunrise Pantoum with a Shrinking Sister 48

T

TABLE 1 34
Teaching Years 62
Thanksgiving Break 46
Thinking I Can Drive after Clearing
   the Snow off Only My Windshield 37

W

Wall Art, Reframed 21
Watching a Man Examine the Prehistoric
   Human Skeleton in the Window of
   the Conference Room I'm In 32
When I First Meet My Paternal Grandaunt
   as an Adult, She Tells Me My Favorite Family
   Recipe Came from Their Childhood Maid 39

First Line Index

Numbers
    7 servings per household 43

A
    a Gertrude Stein poem, which is to say 26
    Analysis of Levels of Parentification 34
    Ask the finches: what else is there 68
    As soon as I stop, everything I hadn't 37
    as we wheeled Mommom 18
    At first, it looks like razed trees, dying 58
    At the cafe, the owner is asked 61
    At the party, I'm a jukebox.
        lOne shot of tequila, another story 25

B
    Bills pile like leaves. Three jobs
        should be enough. At the lake 57

E
    Everything looks bigger in the winter 48
    Every year, in winter, I hear the same sounds 16

H
    He said we'd rename every dog we saw 65
    He sees two geese still on the pond 14
    How will plastic 32

I
    I look most like Sailor Jupiter,
        but I only have brown eyes. I 29
    In the back of the classroom 54
    In the crumbling heart 62
    I think about the way Jess found
        Greg's body dead in front of my 50
    It seems grand—the fondue 67

L
    Like the cop who gets excited 51
    Love is a nostalgia aloof 55

M
    Mermaid eyes. A margarita's iridescent 72
    Mom told us the story of the family
        that raised her mother. The 11
    Multidimensional, needing no introduction 63
    My dad loves giving gifts, making
        the people he loves happy. He 44
    My mom puts on make up, and she is not my mom 42
    My mother's grief 45
    my poems. The flies are more interested 38
    my stepmom sees all three of her sleeping children 20

P
    Patio: Every day I watch my 19
    Poppy died last year, so now I
        re-frame the landscapes, the stories 21

S
    SELFISH 31
    shows me the picture 39
    Some are willing to trust any anchor 23
    Sun steeped in a cup of sky 28

T

"The average dream is a nightmare" 64
The kids eat boredom like snacks 46
The pupils of the purple coneflowers 60
The room is a curly mind, frizzy-brain
    girl like me. It's got a big 59
The sun has a tantrum, throws 41
The trees shake loose 66
The trees swab the clouds. The sky 69
Toxic masculinity says that flexing 70
TRAUMA TRAUMA TRAUMA 53

W

Was I born the mineral 36
We fell asleep in New York, woke up 52
We make do 17
We were all planetary, too 27
When I am close enough, I am reminded 15
When the phone rang 22
White crayons, he says as we wake. *White* 30
Whole and indivisible. A stone pillar 33

Y

You were the window 24

www.ingramcontent.com/pod-product-compliance
Lightning Source LLC
Chambersburg PA
CBHW010047094426
42735CB00020B/3415